TEXTING MEN:

TEXTING SECRETS FOR GIRLS - 7 SIMPLE STEPS TO ATTRACT A MAN AND MAKE ANY GUY OBSESS OVER YOU

BY

Felicia Vine

INTRODUCTION

With the advent of social media, dating and relationships have been taken to a whole new level. Our communication, flirting and even pre-date screening is being done online. These devices were really only meant to make communication easier and faster when we couldn't be around each other, the inventors couldn't have known that they would change the face of dating and relationships forever.

We can never go back. There are some pros and cons to this, as with everything, but the way we communicate over text, email and social media has to change. There is a world of trouble caused by miscommunication, but we can get around that and work it to our advantage.

And this is where you become a master of the language of love, through text.

Table of Contents

LEGAL NOTES

LEARNING THE MIND OF A MAN. YOU CAN'T TALK TO THEM IF YOU DON'T KNOW THEIR LANGUAGE. INCLUDES YOUR FIRST TEXT LESSON.

Let me preface this by saying that men are inherently simple creatures. Women are the more complex ones. This is extremely important to understand, especially in our communication with them. To add insult to injury, communicating through text is even more different.

But, with a few simple rules of thumb, you'll understand what to do. I will warn you though—it won't feel natural to all of you. This is because learning to communicate with a man in a way he will understand is very different than the way women communicate with each other.

The way he reads your tone and body language is far different than the way women mean it. And if you don't think that applies in texting, e-mail or social media, then think again. Your tone can be misunderstood even more, as he can't hear your voice inflections.

Here we will teach you how to get around the voice and tone issues. But first let's go a little deeper into the way he thinks. This way you'll fully understand why we are asking you to text what we are asking you to text, and how. So, ready to have fun?!

MAN + COMMUNICATION = FUN AND SIMPLICITY

Ladies, we've been told time and time again—those old cliché's about the men in our lives and about men in general. If you feed him and have sex with him—he's happy. Now, of course, this is a blanket statement, We can't assume every gent is the same—but we can say that the vast majority have a lot in common in this realm. The same simplicity should be added to texting him.

You've sent your best and most witty text and his answer is a caveman-like "k". Yeah, the only reason why you didn't get the "ugg" was because he was holding a beer with the other hand and couldn't finish the words. And you DON'T relinquish the beer to text a girl...

Men have these unwritten rules that even they don't notice—it's just second nature! But you, the girl, get the silly brunt of it. And when you finally fume enough to get the words out to tell him what an insensitive lug he is—your face to face conversation kind of goes like this.

You—"Really? I give you the best text I had in me and that's all I get?"

Him—"Huh? What did I do?" (If he's intelligent enough he MIGHT grace you with that question, but "Huh" is about par for the course.)

You—(Walk away with an eye roll and less of an understanding of the male animal than you had before)

So, they're just stupid then—end of book...?

The answer is a resounding NO! In fact, this is a sign he's using his brain for what he's supposed to. Remember, he's made for a certain purpose, just like you—just a different purpose. We'll touch on that now, as it pertains to communication, but it can fill a whole other book entirely—and it just might!

Why do they act the way they do?

A man, like a woman, has a brain that is wired to specific purposes. This is a purely scientific statement and has no bearing on whether we are equal as humans. But first, we must understand and accept that we are here, at least in part, to procreate and continue the race together. So, we naturally have urges, thought processes and emotions that are directly related to this. There is no right or wrong in the process.

So, how does this pertain to male communication?

The male of the species is the one that is wired to solve problems in a specific way—quickly and efficiently. To him, conversation is a "functional and practical tool" so words mean less to him than they do to a woman. Why? Because he is always looking for an instruction, or to be moved in a quick and meaningful way.

This is where women get tripped up. What's meaningful is different to him than to a woman. Meaningful to him means "OK, get to the point so I can 'fix' or solve whatever it is you need." So a text message that has nothing but emotions in it is going to be lost on him. Not to say that guys don't like the occasional I love you text, or that they are devoid of emotion, it just serves no real purpose to explain things to him or try to come up with a brilliant line. After a while it gets old and if he's intelligent he'll know you're way too into him or trying too hard and be less challenged by you.

Other than instructions, men love to be needed and feel valuable as well as sexy and desired. This is directly tied into their need for instruction. How can they please you? How do you feel about them? Just don't show him too much—he needs to be challenged.

Text Lesson One

KISS—Keep It Stupidly Simple!

For the first lesson we're going to just teach you his language. You can use these BUT please don't start too much until you've read and digested the rest of the book. Why? Because there is a formula for when and how to use certain texts—we want you to have the best shot at winning so hang in there. This is not rocket science—it's easy and fun.

Texts that showcase what KISS means:

"Thinking of you... That's all"

- Ask a "specific" question—Do you have? Do you want? Are you going here? But never ask questions like—what do you think? How do you feel about?

  All of this is an insignificant enigma to a man and will get you thrown off badly when he says—"I don't know?"

  A man very rarely knows what he thinks of something or how he feels about something until he is forced by circumstance to think about it, and you can't do that for him. You can encourage it, but that is in the following chapters.

- Give him direct choices, like "Do you want Chinese or Pizza?" If you ask him "What do you want for dinner tonight?"—Well, you should be able to fill in the blank by now. Just in case you still aren't clear—the question would be met with "I don't know".

- Ask direct but open ended questions. If it's something he can answer yes or no to the conversation will stall, because he won't see the value in continuing. In his mind—the question is answered. He has no clue that you are inviting him to a conversation.

Chapter 2

TEXTING THE NEW GUY. WHO MAKES THE FIRST MOVE AND WHY?

There is no more confusing time than when you meet a new guy and don't know when to text, or even if you should. Not to mention, you also have to worry about what you text. Now, before we get into your next text lesson, we will cover a few things. You may find it to be a little confusing, just don't overthink it.

When it comes down to it, there really should be no hard and fast rule about how to communicate with anyone—including a man you are romantically interested in. Why? Because if you are an emotionally balanced, mature female with a life, there shouldn't be an issue. If he judges you, he isn't for you anyway. But—somehow—even the most high-powered, intelligent women lose their senses and their confidence when they meet someone they are interested in.

They go against their better judgment and they mess it up. Studies have shown that a high percentage of women admit to being confused about whether to make the first move, and that includes electronic communication.

The most common reason is that they have to be in a traditionally masculine role all day at work, and they are so used to taking control that they find it hard not to do that with a man. They also admit that because they spend so much time trying to impress the higher ranked men they work with they find themselves struggling with self-worth issues. This results in over-compensating and trying a bit too hard. Sometimes they don't realize they were doing this until they look back after the demise of a relationship.

See, the issue is that you can get away with ANYTHING if you are confident. But when we are emotionally vulnerable we sometimes lose that edge. That's why it's confusing for some women. They watch other women get away with it and most times these women are less attractive or less intelligent and they work miracles.

Well, this does nothing but exacerbate the confidence situation with them. So, since confidence can't be taught, we are going to give you the safest guidance we can. The structure will help and your experience will teach you a lot. As you find confidence building techniques—and yes we will give you those too—it will get easier to wean yourself off the texting rules to some degree. But we'll start with the basics.

TEXTING RULES FOR NEW GUYS:

You've met someone incredible. For the first time in a long time your heartbeat skips and you find yourself thinking about him all day long. You have the normal signs of infatuation. Your hands get damp, you can't eat, and you can't sleep. So, what do you do? You just met at Starbucks or online, you've had a few conversations—you exchanged numbers under the guise of business. You don't know if it was an excuse to get your number or if it was a friendly gesture. You don't know his personal situation but there was no date planned. In fact, he hasn't initiated contact, but all you can think about is talking to him again. You're a grown woman, yet you are confused about what to do. So, here's the advice that gives you the best shot.

- **Who Initiated?** If you are the one that gave him your number then it is still acceptable to text him. But since the situation is a gray area and you aren't sure how he feels about you or if he just gave you his number to be polite, you want to make sure your text is not giving him too much. This brings us to point number 2.

- **The Nature of your Text:** First—wait at least 3-5 days before texting. This may be killing you but you won't be in danger of losing your chance in a couple of days, even if he's dating someone casually. Your first text should be no more than 10 words.

Make it a direct question and don't be insulted or say anything about it if he doesn't text back right away, or if he texts back "who is this?" He may not have stored your number, which probably means he's not mad about you, but give it a chance. There could be many reasons for this, but that is not for you to think about

It will stress you out and tempt you to do something stupid—like ask him how he feels or why he didn't store your number. You want to show you're interested by sending a text, but you don't want to come off desperate. Your text could be "haven't been to Starbucks lately—how's your week going?" Wait until he engages. Do NOT text him again. Do NOT follow up on your own texts.

- **Believe that he got the text:** Women LOVE to fool themselves into believing he didn't get the text. They obsess about it so much that they end up popping and texting him—again! Trust that it went through. Most people don't even call anymore—they text.

This means that people are very adept at picking up their texts. The bottom line is—he will text you if he's interested. One way not to worry too much is to choose a couple of guys that interest you—this way you aren't obsessed over one person.

- **If he engages:** If he texts you—don't send another one right away, especially if he was short and answered in one word answers, or cut you off to say he couldn't talk or that he would call you or text later. Again, there could be a million reasons for this but it is not your job to try and figure it out.

This means just get on with life. If he doesn't get to you in a week, then sorry sister—forget him. He may have things going on in his life—you don't know him and you don't need to ask. He may then feel pressured and you don't want him to be polite just to not hurt your feelings. Guys are sort of cowards when it comes to expressing honest feelings to people they don't know—especially girls.

- **Asking Him Out:** We said earlier that it was acceptable for you to ask him out when you asked him for his number—this was not as simple as we made it sound. That's why we left this point out until after the above scenarios. Generally, the feel of the texts you've been getting or the lack thereof will dictate whether you do this or not.

Now, if you've gotten a favorable result, we suggest sending a flirty text at this time. If you've spoken back and forth he may just think he's in the friend or business/networking zone. So, sending a text like. "Ya know, whenever I think of you, it's the darnedest thing, I always remember how blue your eyes are lol I'm kind of a sucker for baby blues" Leave it at that. Now, any guy who is interested should at that time ask you out. If he doesn't but he's flirting back then this is critical, so listen up.

This could mean a few things that you won't want to involve yourself in. First let's get the inappropriate stuff out of the way. He's flirting back and getting personal. Talking about sex or eluding to it or even sending you inappropriate pics. For example it could go down like this. "Well, if you like my eyes you'll really love this" and you get a pic of something you really didn't need to see at this point—or in this way. You need to cut him off immediately and NOT make excuses as to why he did that. Unless you were talking about his body parts only a complete ass**** will react like that. Cut him off or risk getting used—or heaven forbid worse.

The second thing you need to know is that a guy will take the opportunity to flirt and flirt simply because it's fun and you're new, but he may have someone else OR just not be interested. Maybe he's a player and wants to see if he can score but has no interest in dating you—or anyone else for that matter.

The third scenario is he starts texting you and you engage in long conversations. He never asks you out—yet he pops in and out of your phone life. Well, I hate to burst your bubble but this dude is bored and you are the time killer—maybe even his head shrink. Yeah, guys don't bond by talking, they bond with shared experiences—sorry. Women get tripped up by this constantly because you feel he is getting into you and is just bonding away. But, he's probably killing time while taking someone else out. You've been a great psychiatrist though—congrats! Not...

So, now you know the safety zone and the pitfalls. You now know who to cut off and why. Now that we've gotten over the jerk zone and saved your dignity, we're gonna move on to chapter 3 and pretend he was awesome and asked you out (or you him) because he was flirting and drew you in!

Chapter 3

WHEN YOU'RE DATING. WHAT'S APPROPRIATE AND WHAT ISN'T—INCLUDING SEXTING

So, you've made it through the texting dilemma. You finally went on a date. It went great. You laughed, the banter between you was sensational and the kiss was scintillating. You immediately woke your BFF up to tell her the entire thing. Who are you kidding—she was up hoping you posted on Facebook. No such luck—you were having too great a time hanging on every word your date was saying.

Then, one day goes by, and you're cool with it. Two days go by and you're curious but confused about what to do. Three days go by—you are now starting to question yourself. Did he meet someone else? Did you scare him off? Did he drop dead? Did he think about the date and decide you suck? Well, here's how this goes.

A guy can have a great date with a girl and actually scare himself. Guys also have a better talent than gals for staying in the moment. Yeah it's important for you to know this—so listen up... again.

A woman will sit and stare down her date while he's talking—she will be fantasizing about what their children will look like. He, on the other hand, will be enjoying the moment. And we'll tell you what else. He has absolutely NO thought of what your lives may be like together, no matter how wonderful you are. No matter how good you are in bed—he may be thinking about that though—in fact it's a safe bet. He doesn't even know if you are getting a second date yet, let alone an exclusive relationship. Now, this is in fact a typical guy—there are exceptions that are the complete opposite.

If you've found one—congrats—but they aren't a dime a dozen. You probably won't be able to stand outside and throw a rock and hit one. So, we'll treat this as if he's your average Joe.

We aren't just going to tell you how to text him—we're going to give you the secret to giving yourself the best shot at him texting you first, and maybe asking for another date!

The secret is simple—stay in the now. Be a good listener and completely present on your date.

Guys aren't stupid. They have a great sense of knowing. Their radar is good because they aren't clouded by the things women will think about during a date. So, they can tell, at least subconsciously that you are not totally present. It's a turn-off.

He may not know why he doesn't want a second date, he just won't. That text you're waiting for? Well, he's just not driven to do it. Once a guy is turned off there is rarely any going back. So be present. Don't try so hard. Laugh naturally and listen.

Post Date Texting: What's appropriate and what's not.

If the date went really well, you'll be talking. If he's asked for another date either before your last date ended or by text at some point afterward, you need to keep it in balance. In other words, you need to be sure to avoid some of the common pitfalls that many women hit at this point.

You may feel so comfortable talking to him that you've created—in your mind—the "instant relationship". Rest assured, he hasn't. So, don't text him like you're in a relationship yet. If he is the rare kind and is all excited—and this also happens a lot—make sure you respond to him appropriately.

Examples:

- Guys seem to like texting you "Good Morning" or "I hope you have a great day!" This tells you that you are on his mind. BUT please, please, please do NOT get it into your head that you have a boyfriend. What do you do when he does this? Smile, feel good, place no expectation on it and text him back appropriately. Good morning thanks [wink icon]. That would be appropriate.

  Sending a seductive pic or a kiss icon would not be. If HE begins sending inappropriate things then cut him off. If he sends a kiss icon, don't send the same thing back. Send a blushing or a happy icon. If you only have access to a smiley—send him 3 together :-) :-) :-) this way you are flirting back but not just being polite. He will be more intrigued by why you didn't send a kiss back. But he will still know you are interested. You get what's happening right? Now you are a light challenge. You want him to want to see you again because he can't think of anything else. You don't want him to become bored because you respond in kind all the time.

- Between Dates: As we mentioned earlier, he may start out all excited. Especially if he hasn't engaged physically yet. This is a good thing if you haven't engaged in sex. Again, with oodles of true confidence you could get away with it, but no—we are helping the ones who don't quite have it down yet and that's okay.

So, what do you do? At this point, if there are regular texts from him, continue to text appropriately in response until the second date. If you are already past the second date, and you think he's really into you, you can now do the more spontaneous texting and enhance his interest. But you have to do this carefully.

Special note: Frequency of texts should only be either in response to him or spontaneously every other day or two! Don't be predictable.

Examples of Texts to Enhance his Interest:

- Guys like to be teased a bit. But, prior to sex you DO NOT use sexually oriented innuendo in your texts.

- The short and unfinished. This is a good one so long as you do it correctly. Send him one that starts a thought without finishing it. For example. "I was just thinking!" This forces him to respond out of curiosity. He may or may not but if he doesn't DO NOT follow up on your own texts, leave it alone and don't bring it up later. If he does answer, it's likely to be with "yeah?" or "what's that?" Leave it for an hour or so.

Then text the second line which would be something like— "about..." [wink icon]. Then leave it. Regardless of what he says to you as a response, leave it about 15 minutes. Then text back something like "what we would look like in..." and then NO MORE. Leave his mind freaking out about "in what"... Even if he responds asking—DO NOT say another word.

If he calls, don't answer. If he asks why you didn't answer just giggle and say—"well, I was busy silly that's why I texted you!" Just keep the response short, flirty and lighthearted. DO NOT do this more than every few days so the game doesn't get old. If he really likes you, that text will be in his head for a week and in his subconscious for a long, long time.

- **The Elusive Response:** This one has to be done very strategically. Why? Because though it is a game, you want it to remain a positive game and not a negative turnoff. Positioning and timing is everything. Again, this is pre-sex so you don't want to act as if you are a couple yet because in his mind you aren't, even after sex takes place.

When he texts you, he may ask you what you're doing or more like "what's up?" Don't text back right away, wait about 15 minutes and say "Hey there, just running around" NEVER say you're doing nothing even if you haven't gotten out of your pajamas all day. Don't get long winded or specific about what you're doing and how your day went, even if it was a most productive one. Why? Because you don't want to give him a pattern of behavior yet.

Note: The only thing you DON'T get flaky or inconsistent with is your interest in him. If he detects this—he will move on. The "act like you hate him one day and like you love him the next" never comes to anything good—not with a good guy.

The only time that mojo works is when it's a player. And those men you DON'T want. Here's a little education as to why it works on a player. Because the player is challenged by the chase for sex and that is that. Or by getting you to want him. Once he's done that—his job is done and he'll move on.

In the next chapter we will provide you with texts you should always have with you—programmed into your phone and why. Then, we move on to after a relationship has started and deepened, so don't stop here! Read on!

Chapter 4

50 Exclusive Text Messages He Wants You To Send

There are text messages that are better to send a man and there are your standard flirty messages that you can take a chance on. But, we've taken it a big step forward and did the research with real men. Yes, men of all ages and backgrounds. We read, asked, studied and came up with a pretty exclusive list of texts that he actually wants you to send. How much better can you get than that?

STOP! We need to preface this before we begin. These are a vast mix of texts to keep in your collection. Some of them will be for now when he's new and others will be for when you've had sex and others will be for when you have a relationship. Just read them, store them and don't use the ones that DO NOT have an asterisk * next to them until you finish the book. We put this list in this chapter so you could use SOME right NOW but NOT ALL. Why not get ahead of the game right away. Just don't get CARRIED away!

1. Ordering Chinese, fried or white rice? *
2. I'm horny—what you waiting for?
3. Let's skip the party and watch a movie
4. Let me help you out with Valentine's Day, X mas or any holiday. Here is a list of gifts at a reasonable price. Pick any one of them and I'm happy.
5. Last night was AMAZING
6. My parents couldn't make it so we dodged that bullet till next year!
7. OMG can you believe what happened in _____ show you both watched together recently? *
8. Nah, you don't need to call me tonight. Go out with the guys! *
9. Oh, for future reference, my dress/bra size is.
10. Can't wait for tonight! *

11. Surprise! I got us 2 tickets to the Lakers!
12. [Dirty picture]
13. You are the funniest guy out of all your friends *
14. Oh I'm not jealous of her, I know you're great friends, not worried
15. She's pretty hot—still want that threesome.
16. I'm ready when you are! (and really be ready) *
17. My parents really do like you.
18. Just bought the most amazing thongs. How about a runway show.
19. Yeah, I noticed you staring down her rack. You're a guy, I totally get that you find other women hot. Totally OK. *
20. I don't find Brad Pitt attractive at all actually *
21. Just a night out with the gals—no guys allowed.
22. I'm on my period this week. Not really myself—let's hang out when it's done. *
23. I have NO desire for marriage right now!*
24. You were so hot yesterday! *
25. Hope you enjoyed your night! I left you some coffee and aspirin in the kitchen (only if you are dating and staying the night or living with him please, otherwise you are a stalker)
26. Get up! I made breakfast and yes there's bacon! (Living with him only)
27. Been thinking of you all day *
28. Hey no problem. Focus on all the work you have to do and we'll hang out when you're done! *
29. Screw the diet for tonight—let's eat whatever you want. *
30. Hey, just to remind you that your mom's got a birthday coming up next week.
31. If you tell me what turns you on—we'll do it tonight!
32. I'm not gonna get plastered tonight I swear, no 2am drunk call. *
33. It's cool if you don't wanna hang with my clan tonight—I totally understand. *
34. LOL I can't believe I'm saying this but you are WAY bigger than my ex. It left an impression, I just had to say something.
35. I'll bring the handcuffs, you bring the condoms—come on over!
36. Go watch the game with your friends—I just wanna chill tonight.
37. Just spoke to a buddy of mine. He may have a job for you!
38. Tonight, it's all about you baby! *
39. Relax, I took care of the housework!
40. I'm cooking so what do you fancy for dinner tonight?
41. I'm paying—where do you wanna eat tonight? *

42. Nah, I don't want to see some chick flick tonight. Let's do some action adventure. *
43. No actor could ever hold a candle to you baby! *
44. You are way too hot for the gym. *
45. I LOVE your friends they are so much fun to hang with! *
46. My friends really think you are totally cool. *
1. 47.You know, when you _____that really turns me on!
47. I'm so sorry you were right
48. I really don't care about grandiose and expensive romantic gestures, it's a waste of money. *
49. I totally loved that song you asked me to listen to! *

So, now you have a targeted arsenal of texts to use. Remember to only use the ones with the asterisk when you are new and not engaging in sex. If you have slipped or decided to have sex early, we advise you to pull back a bit. This is because we don't want you to assume a relationship. Remember, we said that a guy will not typically assume relationship status even after sex, and especially with early sex.

Believe it or not, most women think guys are emotionally immature for not assuming a relationship after sex. But let's shift your perspective a little. If he is treating you like an adult with the assumption that you are 50% of the equation—willingly—then wouldn't it be emotionally immature to assume relationship status when he barely knows you?

Now we move on to the next chapter.

Chapter 5

How to Keep Yourself Out of the "Just For Sex" and the "Just Friends" Zones

In the previous chapters you got a pretty good education not only on texts to use and when, and the ones best saved for special times. You also got a look into a man's mind, which is a valuable piece of knowledge. You were given 50 awesome texts of varying styles that you can use to make sure you have the best shot at getting it down the first time.

In this chapter we are giving you the best insight on how to stay out of the two most painful zones a girl can suddenly find herself in, without even realizing. The unfortunate thing is, they invite this behavior. Let's get into a little bit of why. It's no good to just tell you what not to do.

Why? Because every behavior has a basis in something, and that something should be addressed in order to get the best out of it. Most times when a woman puts herself in a situation such as the "just for sex" role or the "just friends zone" she could have several issues or a motive but is unwittingly taking the wrong action. This action takes her nowhere near the result she intended.

The Just for Sex Role:

Let's take a look at how a woman would put herself in this role. She sends a naked pic, or thinks she's being seductive and more conservative and sends a pic in her pajamas etc... Her intention is to get him attracted to her. She has succeeded in a way—unfortunately though, not in the way she intended. She is then flattered by the attention and the compliments she gets on how sexy she is and how much he keeps thinking about her.

But once the cork is popped, so to speak, and sex—even virtual sex—has been had, the party is over. One of two things generally happens in this case. He uses her as a masturbation tool because from the first naked, PJ or sext text, she is in the "just for sex" zone. He will meet her but never date her. She will believe she's something special and get left in the dirt to dry up with all the past women that have engaged with him.

So, men are just jerks then?

Uh, no. Some are, but you also have to take responsibility for your part in it as well, for your own good and your future with men. This happens in part because there are other complicated factors that come with each personality. But for now we'll stick with the basics.

We said earlier that men are simple creatures for a reason. Because they hunt, provide, fix and solve... period. When they process information with the emotional and the reptilian side of the brain, they will process what you give them at face value.

If it looks like a duck, quacks like a duck and walks like a duck, it must be a duck. If you look like you want sex, act like you want sex and text like you want sex—then his common sense will tell him that you want sex. A man wants nothing more than to please and satisfy. So, when you send sexts or sexy pics he gets more into it and more graphic. There are women out there that will straight up get offended. Why? He's just following your lead!

So, what have we learned? Men make inferences based on being visual and literal creatures. So, how do you avoid this scenario? NO SEXTS BEFORE A RELATIONSHIP. That also means NO SEXTS AFTER SEX if there is not a relationship first.

Why? Because if there is no VERBAL asking of a relationship by one of you, all you've done is sent him the wrong message in a sext and sealed your "Just for Sex" fate with physical sex before you are in relationship.

How to use his nature to your advantage:

Using texts to use his visual and literal nature to your advantage is simple. In the 50 texts with the asterisks that we gave you in chapter four there is language that actually draws on his primal instinct to chase what he does not yet have.

BUT, listen up good here, OK?

Those texts appeal to the correct side of his brain that is going to chase **YOU** *and* **NOT** *just your* **ASS***. There is a difference.*

OK now that we've gotten the hardest part through your head we can balance the other extreme and keep you out of the "just friends zone".

Come to think of it, we might add another more subtle zone here. You can text yourself into the "friend" zone and then slide into the "friend with benefits zone". Now, how is that different from the "just for sex zone"? Easy, it's worse. Not only are you there when he needs a sexual release—you're there to be his personal psychologist and his personal time killer.

Then, he comes to you to talk about... You guessed it—advice on how to win over some chick he really wants to date! Oh the horror!

So, let's keep you out of this one too. Here's how to do it.

Change your view on texting:

It's bad enough that no one calls anymore, but to add insult to injury, you can easily put yourself in a compromising position while texting. There are people who carry on virtual relationships via text, and the most they have to offer is an occasional Skype date. Technology is an amazing thing, but it can get you into trouble if you view it as something it's not.

Texting is there for short and sweet words that are functional and make life convenient. Like, "on my way" or "got stuck at the house, leaving now". After all, texting contributes to both convenience and safety, as well as allowing you to better keep track of your kids.

But texting has appealed to the laziness in all of us. To be successful we need to be emotionally mature enough to view of texting for what it is. Here are a few tips to keep you out of all those zones we talked about, and work on having a great relationship.

Tips for keeping you out of the bad zones:

- Refuse to have a conversation via text and keep your phone conversations to 20 minutes tops. Be honest or maybe just a little white lie and tell him you aren't much of a phone person. A quality guy will get that and will be texting you to ask you out rather than using you because you're conveniently there.

  Of course, if he has a family tragedy or something, let him talk as long as he needs. BUT a tragedy doesn't mean ongoing personal drama with his buddies or family or anything. Remember—you aren't his psychologist.

- We already know the sexting and naked rule. Make sure you keep to flirting and compliments, not sex talk of any kind.

- Don't be there just when he's bored. If he has a habit of texting "what's up?" and there is no real purpose, text back once and then be busy. Do not be his time killer. Guys like to text people when they are bored, so if you allow him to count on you to be there, change that. Don't be.

So, now we are done with the new guy and the just dating. But what about when you've been in a relationship for a while? You need to spice things up a bit? In the next chapter we are going to look at some of those texts from chapter 4 that you can use in your already great relationship!

Chapter 6

30 EXAMPLES OF HOW TO SPICE UP AN EXISTING RELATIONSHIP WITH TEXTING.

* I'm horny—what you waiting for?

* Let's skip the party and watch a movie

* Let me help you out with Valentine's Day, X-mas or any other holiday. Here is a list of gifts at a reasonable price. Pick any one of them and I'm happy.

* Last night was AMAZING

* Can't wait for tonight!

* Surprise! I got us 2 tickets to the Lakers!

* [Dirty picture]

* You are the funniest guy out of all your friends

* Just bought the most amazing thongs. How about a runway show?

* Yeah, I noticed you staring down her rack. You're a guy, I totally get that you find other women hot. Totally okay.

* I'm on my period this week. Not really myself—let's hang out when it's done.

* You were so hot yesterday!

* Hope you enjoyed your night! I left you some coffee and aspirin in the kitchen

* Get up! I made breakfast and yes there's bacon! [Living with him only]

* Been thinking of you all day

* Screw the diet for tonight—let's eat whatever you want.

* Hey, just to remind you that your mom's got a birthday coming up next week.

* If you tell me what turns you on—we'll do it tonight!

* I'll bring the handcuffs, you bring the condoms—come on over!

* Go watch the game with your friends—I just wanna chill tonight.

* Tonight, it's all about you baby!

* Relax, I took care of the house work!

* I'm cooking so what do you fancy for dinner tonight?

* I'm paying—where do you wanna eat tonight?

* Nah, I don't want to see some chick flick tonight.

* Let's do some action adventure.

* No actor could ever hold a candle to you baby!

* You know when you _____ that really turns me on!

* I'm so sorry you were right

* I really don't care about grandiose and expensive romantic gestures, it's a waste of money.

The above texts are ones you can use to spice up a marriage or an already ongoing committed relationship. Believe it or not, some of these are really needed in an existing relationship. You want to be able to rediscover each other.

Studies have shown that, biologically speaking, we aren't meant to stay together without work for an extended period of time. Especially after we have kids and they are of a responsible age. So the more we use tools like text to bring the spark back the better off we all are.

So, what happens when we break up and there are regrets? Can we use text to get our ex back? The last chapter is devoted to just that.

TEXTING BACK THE EX

Let's preface this by saying that your ex is your ex for a reason. Unless you are one of those people that breaks up after a little fight and then it's on again. This is an issue in and of itself and may be another book. And it's also a personality issue that needs to be addressed. Again, another book.

The way you set yourself up for success is you have to not do anything at all for the first 30 days. Yup, sorry, there are things your ex needs to go through as a guy and regardless of who dumped who, you've got to give him the space he needs in order for the text to work. You are creating a great opportunity to maximize the text. Doing anything emotional or premature is relationship suicide.

- Wait 30 days. That's 4 weeks. Guys always believe you'll be calling any minute because you can't stand being away. Even if they dumped you, it's an ego booster to have you falling all over them. Don't give in. When you finally wham them with a text your impact will be sensational.

- Text him a happy text. Nothing about the breakup and no apologies or dissertations. For example—"I just came back from _____, remember that amazing date we had there and we laughed all night? Just made me think of you and smile really."

- Wait for him to react. And unless he asks if it's OK if he calls you or is it OK if he sees you then don't text back. If he doesn't respond, don't text again. Sometimes these things just don't work out. There is no guarantee and each person has different circumstances. We can't cover them all.

So, if he does ask for you to come back, act as if you aren't sure but you are willing to talk. Allow him to be the pursuer this time, especially if you are the one who was dumped. Don't initiate contact again. Let him come to you, and you respond. But, the main idea is NOT to bring up the circumstances surrounding the breakup. You want to associate yourself with good feelings. This is the only way back into his heart and his life.

- The most important thing is you don't ask him to get together and you don't bring up the relationship. Right now, you're only texting and warming up to each other again. This can take some time because everyone is gun shy. If you dumped him, he may still suffer from a bruised ego. If he dumped you—you don't want to be the beggar.

And believe us when we say that you can come off that way without even mentioning the breakup or apologizing. The point is that you are still forming a rapport with each other as if you just met. It's better that way. This way you are like a new woman to him, while hooking him back with good memories.

- Never try to convince. When you are mentioning memories, the last thing you want to do is to say things afterward to mess it up like "don't you want it to be that way again". Leave it alone at the good memory and let him sit a while with it. If he's really interested, he will eventually react.

CONCLUSION

We are so glad you took the right action in reading this book. We hope your dating experience and your life in general has been enriched as well as your knowledge of the male mind. We intended to give you balanced and thorough information, and wanted to make sure you were getting more than just a list of texts. We don't believe in giving lists with no explanation. Words rarely teach, but examples do. Please feel free to let us know what you thought!

ABOUT THE AUTHOR

Felicia Vine is an author & relationship expert, born in Italy in a small city called Otranto. At 16 she moved to the USA with her parents, where she graduated from the University of Rochester with degree in psychology.

Now she is working as a relationship consultant and freelance writer, writing articles on relationship topics for several online resources.

In her spare time, Felicia writes books to enlighten the public on relationship and sex topics. She has also authored several romance and erotica novels.

Now she lives in New York with her boyfriend and small Yorkshire terrier, Allie.

CAN I ASK A FAVOUR?

Word-of-mouth is crucial for any author to succeed. If you enjoyed this book, found it useful or otherwise then I'd really appreciate it if you would post a short review on Amazon. I do read all the reviews personally so that I can continually write what people are wanting:

Thanks for your support!

Printed in Great Britain
by Amazon